937
R

90-454

Rosen, Mike

The journeys of Hannibal

Harford Day School

Bel Air, Maryland

THE JOURNEYS OF
HANNIBAL

Mike Rosen

Illustrated by Tony Smith

The Bookwright Press
New York · 1990

Great Journeys

The Conquest of Everest
The Expeditions of Cortés
The First Men on the Moon
The First Transatlantic Flight
The First Voyage Around the World
The Journey to the North Pole
The Journeys of Hannibal
The Race to the South Pole
The Travels of Marco Polo
The Voyage of Columbus
The Voyage of the Beagle

First published in the
United States in 1990 by
The Bookwright Press
387 Park Avenue South
New York, NY 10016

First published in 1990 by
Wayland (Publishers) Limited
61 Western Road, Hove
East Sussex BN3 1JD, England

Library of Congress Cataloging-in-Publication Data
Rosen, Mike.
  Hannibal / by Mike Rosen.
    p. cm.
  Includes bibliographical references.
  Summary: Recounts the life of the
Carthaginian military genius and his
army's journey from North Africa across
the Alps to Italy in an attempt to defeat
the Roman Empire.
  ISBN 0–531–18334–3
  1. Hannibal—Juvenile literature. 2.
Punic War, 2d, 218–210 B.C.—Juvenile
literature. 3. Generals—Tunisia—
Carthage (Ancient city)—Biography—
Juvenile literature. [1. Hannibal. 2.
Generals.] I. Title.
DG249.R67 1990
937′.04′092—dc20
[B]   89–36791
[92]   CIP
                                    AC

Typeset by DP Press Ltd, Sevenoaks, Kent
Printed in Italy by G. Canale & C.S.p.A., Turin

Cover *Hannibal's journey to Rome has established him as one of the best-known figures in history. His passage across the Alps, on which his army was accompanied by a group of elephants, was filled with danger and adventure.*

Frontispiece *Hannibal was born in 247 BC. He was the son of the great Carthaginian leader Hamilcar Barca and was sworn at an early age to hate everything to do with Rome and the Roman civilization.*

Contents

Hannibal and Carthage

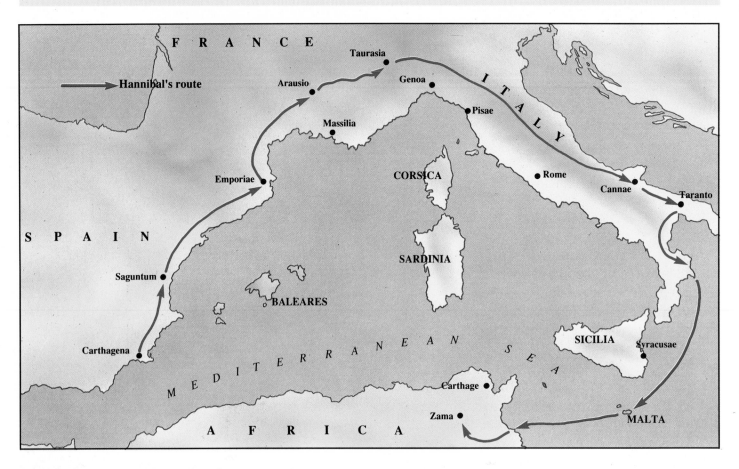

In the darkened Temple of Melkort wisps of smoke hung in the air. Oil lamps and reed torches flickered, casting wild shadows on the walls. Hannibal, just nine years old, stayed close beside his father as they approached the altar. There lay the sacrificed animal. Obeying his father, Hannibal rested his hand on its dead body. Then, as his father listened, Hannibal promised to fight against Rome for as long as he lived.

Hannibal's father, Hamilcar Barca, was one of the richest men in the North African city of Carthage. In 241 BC, Carthage suffered defeat in the war with

the Italian city of Rome. Hamilcar feared that Rome meant to conquer all the lands of North Africa. For this reason he wanted his son Hannibal to be the lifelong enemy of Rome.

Hannibal was born in 247 BC. Hundreds of years before Hannibal's birth, Phoenician traders from the great Levantine city of Tyre had sailed along the coast of North Africa. They built trading posts where the people of the area could meet to buy and sell their goods. One of those towns was Carthage. When the Phoenician Queen Elissa and a group of rich merchants had to flee from Tyre

Above *A map of the western Mediterranean, showing the route Hannibal followed in his long struggle against the Romans.*

in 814 BC they chose Carthage as their new home.

Carthage was well placed to be a trading city. Its sheltered bay provided a safe harbor, and the land around the city was fertile. From Carthage on the North African coast it was a short voyage to Sicily. Only the Straits of Messina lay between Sicily and the main coast of Italy. On reaching the Italian coast, Carthaginian traders could travel easily around the northern shores of the western Mediterranean.

Carthage grew quickly. Merchants explored the coast of Africa as far south as Nigeria. Others turned north at the Straits of Gibraltar, working along the coasts of Spain, Portugal, and western France. Some traders even traveled as far as the southwest shores of Britain. Carthage won control of the Italian coast, and soon the islands of Sicily, Sardinia, and Corsica were ruled by allies of Carthage.

Control of trade in the western Mediterranean brought great wealth to Carthage. By 300 BC the Carthaginians kept a fleet of several hundred war-galleys to protect their merchant ships. The city was surrounded by a massive wall, 20 miles (32 km) long. Within this wall lived 400,000 people. There were two walled harbors; one for merchant ships, and one where war-galleys were built secretly. With their wealth and power the people of Carthage felt safe, but in Italy the strength of Rome was growing.

Above *Hannibal, pictured on a Carthaginian coin from about 220 BC.*

Above *These ruins are all that remain of the once powerful North African state of Carthage.*

New Carthage

After their defeat, the Carthaginians needed to restore their wealth. Although they could no longer control trade with Italy, Carthaginian merchants still traded with Spain and the rest of Africa. Hamilcar Barca was determined to build on these trading links to create a new empire.

Hamilcar had many enemies. Other rich families were jealous of his power and popularity. The merchants of Carthage wanted nothing more than the chance to earn money from trade. Both of these groups opposed Hamilcar's plans for a new empire. They said that Hamilcar wanted to become ruler of Carthage, and that his plans were nothing more than a plot to bring him personal wealth and power.

Despite his enemies, Hamilcar won the trust of the Carthaginian people. He convinced them that Rome would not rest until Carthage was destroyed. They must build an empire powerful enough to challenge the Romans before it was too late. The people of Carthage voted in favor of Hamilcar's plans.

In 238 BC Hamilcar marched with his army along the North African coast toward Spain. With him went his brother Hasdrubal and his son Hannibal who was still a young boy. On their journey they persuaded other cities on the coast to send soldiers with them. They crossed the Straits of Gibraltar with a large army and headed for the city of Gades (present-day Cadiz in Spain).

Above *A 19th-century painting of Cartagena in Spain. Over two thousand years earlier, when it was called New Carthage, this was the main city of Carthage's Spanish empire.*

Above *This coin (c 225 BC) shows the head of Hamilcar Barca, Hannibal's father.*

Gades was a large Carthaginian trading post. Through it came gold from Africa, tin from Britain, and silver from the mines of Spain. For eight years it was Hamilcar's base as he fought to conquer the fierce Spanish tribes. Gradually, Carthaginian rule spread farther into Spain. Then, in 228 BC Hamilcar died.

On Hamilcar's death, Hasdrubal Barca took over as leader of the Carthaginians in Spain. Hasdrubal continued to build the new Carthaginian empire. Instead of fighting the Spanish tribes, he made them allies by helping them in their battle against the Gauls of northern Spain. Eventually he was able to build a great city on the eastern coast of Spain, which he named New Carthage.

It had a fine harbor, and the forests nearby provided the wood for a fleet of warships.

News of Hasdrubal's successes reached the Romans. Afraid of this growing empire, they wanted to limit its size. An agreement was reached that the Carthaginians would not move farther north than the Ebro River. Hasdrubal was happy to agree to this as he needed more time to prepare his army for battle. When he was ready he would break this agreement and attack Rome.

Meanwhile, the new empire was helping the old Carthage to grow strong and wealthy once more. When Hasdrubal was killed in 221 BC, everything was ready for Hamilcar's son Hannibal to take control of the new empire.

Left *A 19th-century view of Carthaginian galleys exploring a strange coast. Most war-galleys would have had several banks of oars and a streamlined shape.*

Hannibal's Plan

Hannibal was twenty-six years old when he became leader of the Carthaginians in Spain. Since leaving Carthage he had lived with the army as it moved from place to place. When Hamilcar and Hasdrubal planned their battles, Hannibal had listened. As he grew older Hannibal fought in many fierce battles and took part in the peace talks between the Carthaginians and Spaniards. He was well trained for the job he had been given.

Hannibal remembered his promise in the Temple of Melkort. For seventeen years he had helped to build the strength of Carthage and the new empire. Now he was ready to carry out the plan he had discussed with Hamilcar and Hasdrubal for the attack on Rome.

The easiest route from Spain to Rome was by sea. For centuries Carthaginian war-galleys had ruled the western Mediterranean, but since the war with Rome they had lost that control. Hannibal could not risk being caught by the Roman fleet before he reached Italy, so he decided to travel overland.

The journey would be difficult. Hannibal and his army would have to find a way through the wild country of Spain, across the mountains of the Pyrenees, and into France.

Left *The Pyrenees mark the modern border between France and Spain. This wild range of mountains was the first major obstacle that Hannibal encountered.*

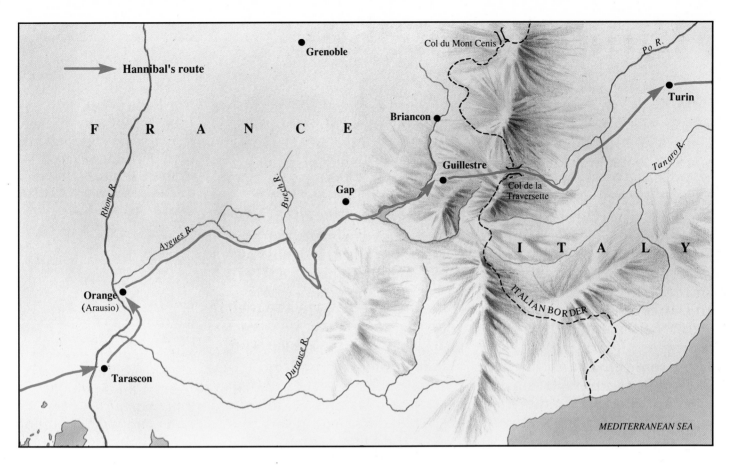

The map shows the following labels:

- Grenoble
- Col du Mont Cenis
- Po R.
- Turin
- Hannibal's route
- Briancon
- F R A N C E
- Guillestre
- Rhone R.
- Buech R.
- Gap
- Col de la Traversette
- Tanaro R.
- Aygues R.
- I T A L Y
- Orange (Arausio)
- Durance R.
- ITALIAN BORDER
- Tarascon
- MEDITERRANEAN SEA

Then they would cross the flooded delta of the Rhone River before reaching the most difficult part of the journey, the crossing of the high mountain passes of the Alps. Crossing the Alps with an army was thought impossible, but Hannibal believed he could do it.

The route overland was 1,500 miles (2,400 km) long. Although some of the army could travel by horse, most of them would have to march on foot. After leaving the lands ruled by Carthage there would be no real roads until they reached Italy. Hannibal and his army would be marching along paths and tracks through forests, plains, and narrow mountain gorges. They would have to cross rivers that had never been bridged, wading through them, swimming, or floating across on rafts. The whole time they would be moving through lands they had never seen, ruled by people who might attack them.

Before he could start his journey, Hannibal had work to do in Spain. He put his brother Hasdrubal in charge of New Carthage, with enough soldiers to defend it if the Romans attacked. To strengthen Carthaginian friendship with the Spaniards, Hannibal married Imilce, the daughter of a powerful chieftain. Finally, he attacked and defeated the town of Saguntum, which lay in Carthaginian lands but was friendly to Rome. Then he gathered his army and began to prepare for his long march.

Above *The exact route that Hannibal took through the Alps has never been found. Some experts disagree about the details, but the route shown in this map fits closely with the information given in the Roman accounts of Hannibal's journey.*

First Steps

Hannibal's army was formed from a mix of many peoples. There were Carthaginian and Spanish footsoldiers, slingers and archers from the Balearic Islands, and cavalry from Numidia. Together they numbered about 100,000 men. To support these soldiers there was a baggage train of wagons and carts to carry tents, food, and supplies. Finally, there were 37 elephants, which had been specially trained for battle. They would charge at the enemy in a great stampede, trumpeting loudly. Horses and soldiers would flee in terror from the path of these massive beasts.

Such a large mass of men could not move quickly, and it was important that they keep together. The baggage train was always protected by the Numidian cavalry.

Where the path was narrow, the distance between the head and rear of the army could be several miles long. At a river crossing, the soldiers would crowd along the banks, waiting to cross.

Every day Hannibal and his army marched from 9 to 12 miles. Each night they wearily set up camp. Hannibal and the other leaders slept in their tents while the soldiers huddled

Far right *When Hannibal's army saw the Pyrenees and learned their destination was Rome, a group of Spanish soldiers refused to go any farther. Hannibal allowed them to return home.*

Below *Hannibal's army consisted of a mixture of people from many different lands. Besides the Carthaginians there were Numidian cavalry and Spanish soldiers. Later, many Gauls joined Hannibal in Italy.*

around the campfires to keep warm. All night long the sentries guarded the edges of the camp from enemy attack.

It took over two months for Hannibal and his army to cross Spain and reach the foothills of the Pyrenees. On the journey they fought many fierce battles against the peoples of the Catalonian mountains. Hannibal was forced to capture several towns and leave some of his soldiers behind to keep these lands under control.

When they reached the Pyrenees, more trouble started. Until this moment, Hannibal had kept his plans secret from most of his army. Many of the soldiers had thought that their goal was to conquer more land for the Carthaginian empire. They had expected to win wealth for themselves from the looting of defeated cities, but now the soldiers learned the truth.

The soldiers listened as Hannibal told them his plan. As they listened they looked at the great mountains of the Pyrenees blocking their path. They heard about the many dangers to come, especially the crossing of the Alps. At the end of their dangerous journey they would have to fight the Roman legions. Some were afraid and others grew angry.

That night the leader of 3,000 Spanish soldiers came to Hannibal. He told Hannibal that his troops would go no farther and demanded that they be paid. Hannibal was afraid mutiny would spread through

the camp. He agreed to the Spaniards' demands and sent them away, together with 7,000 more soldiers who were unhappy with his plans to cross the Alps.

Although Hannibal's army was now much smaller than before, he could totally trust the men who were still with him.

Below *Most of Hannibal's elephants were African, like the ones shown here. He also had a few Indian elephants, which were smaller.*

Mountains and Marshes

Despite their fears, Hannibal and his army crossed the Pyrenees easily. Although snow lay on the peaks, the path across the Col de Perthus was clear. It was midsummer and the valleys were full of lush pastures and wildflowers. The people of the Pyrenees let the army pass peacefully. As they came down into the foothills with the Pyrenees beind them, Hannibal's soldiers felt sure of their success.

Now Hannibal was moving east across the southern lands of France. He followed the line of the coast, moving inland to avoid the big cities. Often his march was stopped by hostile Gauls who were afraid that Hannibal had come to conquer them. Hannibal wanted to cross France without too many battles. His plan was to reach

Below *After crossing the Pyrenees, Hannibal led his army across southern France and through the marshes of the Rhone delta.*

Italy and he could not risk being defeated in France. Usually Hannibal would offer to buy food, horses, or other supplies from the Gauls in return for a safe passage. If that failed, Hannibal would give them money to let him pass. Sometimes the Gauls would not be satisfied, and Hannibal's soldiers would have to fight their way through.

After three weeks' march, Hannibal and his army reached the delta where the Rhone River meets the sea. This was a wild land of treacherous marshes. Floods hid the ground, making it impossible to see where it was safe to tread. Soft bogs, quicksand, and deep mud could trap the soldiers with their heavy loads and armor. A maze of streams and rivers flowed through the swamps making it easy to get lost. Trying to cross the marshes without help from local people would have been impossible.

Hannibal paid local Gauls to guide his army safely through the delta. Then he marched north along the west bank of the Rhone River. About 35 miles (60 km) inland, Hannibal's soldiers reached a place where they could cross. Once again an army of hostile Gauls faced them on the far bank.

Hannibal knew that his army could not cross the river and attack the Gauls without great danger. Boats and rafts would be needed to cross the river safely. Many soldiers would be killed while still in the water or while struggling up the river bank. Hannibal set out to persuade the hostile Gauls to let his army cross without a fight.

Meanwhile, he sent his soldiers to collect all the boats in the area. Others set to work building rafts and carving dugouts from tree trunks. Within a few days, Hannibal had as many boats and rafts as he needed, but the Gauls were still hostile. It was clear that there was going to be a battle.

Across the Rhone

Hannibal planned the battle carefully. A group of Spanish soldiers was sent to cross the river farther north. Two days after crossing the river these soldiers were hiding behind the Gauls' camp. To show Hannibal that they were ready, the Spanish soldiers lit a huge fire. When Hannibal saw the smoke signal, he gave the order for his army to cross the river. The bigger boats crossed upstream of the rafts and dugouts, protecting the smaller craft. On the larger boats some of the cavalry were already seated on their horses, ready to ride into battle as soon as they landed.

When they saw Hannibal's boats on the river, the Gauls gathered on the bank, ready to fight. Suddenly, the Spanish soldiers leaped out of hiding and attacked the Gauls from behind. In the confusion Hannibal's soldiers were able to cross the river safely. Although the Gauls fought hard, Hannibal's soldiers now defeated them easily. With both sides of the river under his control, Hannibal could move the rest of his army across. For

Below *Hannibal could not persuade the Gauls to let him cross the Rhone in peace. In the battle that followed, Hannibal's careful planning helped him to gain a great victory.*

Above *After defeating the Gauls, Hannibal built rafts to carry the elephants across the Rhone.*

two more days the rafts and boats ferried back and forth across the water.

The last to be sent across were the elephants. This was a difficult task as the elephants became terrified. A long ramp was built far out into the river. At the end of this ramp were large rafts. Both the ramp and the rafts were covered with earth to make them look like dry land. The elephants were led along the ramp onto the rafts, which were then ferried across the river. Most of the elephants were fooled by this trick, but some realized what was happening and panicked. As the elephants charged around, the rafts capsized and the animals and their riders fell into the river. Many of the riders drowned, but the elephants kept their trunks above water and walked safely to the shore.

While Hannibal waited for his army to cross the river, he sent his Numidian cavalry to explore the river bank. About 15 miles (25 km) south of Hannibal's camp, the Numidians were attacked by some Romans. The Romans chased the Numidians back to Hannibal's camp. Hannibal guessed that these Romans must be part of a large army. Now that the Romans knew where Hannibal was, they would soon come to find him. He immediately ordered his army to start marching north. When the Romans arrived, Hannibal's camp was empty.

Toward the Mountains

After several days' march Hannibal's army reached a place where another river flowed into the Rhone. A large group of Gauls had gathered there, but after Hannibal helped them to settle an argument they offered to help him. Hannibal asked the Gauls to guide him to the Alps. As they moved toward the mountains the air grew colder, and Hannibal realized he had little time left before winter. He had hoped to be able to cross the Alps in summer but the journey had been harder than he had expected. Hannibal knew he must move fast; to be trapped in the Alpine passes by blizzards would be a disaster.

The Gauls left Hannibal at the foot of the Alps. He gathered his army together and set off toward the first mountain pass. The long line of soldiers, cavalry, baggage animals, and elephants stretched along the valley floor for several miles.

Just before the pass, Hannibal sent scouts ahead to check that the way was safe. They returned with bad news. A group of mountain peoples, the Allobroges, was waiting at the top of the pass ready to ambush Hannibal. He decided to pitch camp and wait. For several days his scouts watched the Allobroges at work. Each morning the Allobroges took positions on either side of the pass, with piles of rocks ready to hurl down the steep slopes onto Hannibal's soldiers. At night they returned to their villages for food and rest.

Hannibal knew what he had to do. Just before dawn he took the best of his Spanish soldiers up the valley. While the Allobroges were still asleep in their villages, Hannibal and his soldiers took control of all of their strongholds.

Below *As his soldiers weakened under the hail of boulders and spears, Hannibal knew he could wait no longer. He led the rest of his army back down the slopes into the battle.*

Through the clear, cold dawn Hannibal's army moved up to the pass and began to cross into the valleys on the other side. The Allobroges watched in fury. When Hannibal's baggage animals began to move, the Allobroges' patience finally ran out. With terrifying war-cries they poured down the slopes, hurling rocks and spears. Their attack was so fierce that Hannibal's soldiers were unable to resist.

Hannibal watched anxiously from the pass as the battle raged. He could not afford to lose his baggage animals and the food they carried. As his soldiers began to retreat, Hannibal could watch no longer. With his well-trained Spaniards, he swept down from the pass. His soldiers below saw him coming to their aid and gained new courage. Squeezed between the two parts of Hannibal's army, the Allobroges stood little chance. The few that escaped fled into the mountains.

Danger in the Alps

As the Allobroges fled, Hannibal led his army through the mountain pass. After a few miles they reached the Allobroges' village. It was empty of people but full of food, cattle, and fuel for fires. Hannibal took advantage of this good luck to replace the supplies that he had lost during the battle.

As they moved higher, the temperature grew ever colder. The massive peaks on each side cast the valleys into shadow for much of the day. The sun could not be seen over the mountains until mid-morning and vanished behind the summits early in the evening. In the mornings the soldiers awoke to find frost glittering on the grass and ice on the path. Many died of cold as they slept.

The Alps seemed to stretch forever. Without local guides it was hard for Hannibal to be sure they were going the right way. The position of the sun by day and the stars by night helped to point the general direction, but it was difficult to follow this over rough ground. After some days they came to a valley where a large river flowed in many streams. Luckily the streams were not too deep and the soldiers could wade across on the stony riverbeds. This time the elephants were happy to walk through the water, and the soldiers pitched camp for a few days' rest in the fertile valley.

Left *High in the Alps huge glaciers slowly grind their way down the valleys, past fertile slopes covered with trees and flowers.*

Below *Many times Hannibal's soldiers had to clear the path where landslides or rockfalls had blocked their way.*

When the army set off again Hannibal's scouts began to bring him worrying reports. The mountain peoples were plucking up courage. They were

gathering in a narrow gorge ahead, where the soldiers would have to pass through in close columns. Before the army reached the gorge, Hannibal placed his best soldiers at the front and rear of the columns. The baggage animals would be well protected because Hannibal kept them in the middle of the columns of men.

Despite Hannibal's careful plans his soldiers were soon in great danger. As they moved through the narrow gorge, massive rocks and boulders were hurled down on them from the cliffs above. Crowded together on the narrow path, the soldiers could not move out of the way. In that first attack the army was split in two with a mass of broken rocks between them.

Then the mountain people came up the gorge behind Hannibal's army. If Hannibal had not put his best soldiers at the rear of the column all his supplies and baggage would have been captured. There was a fierce struggle but at last Hannibal and his soldiers escaped to safety.

Below *Once again Hannibal faced disaster as hostile Gauls bombarded his army with huge rocks. Trapped in the narrow gorge, the Carthaginian soldiers had no space to escape. Hannibal's army was split in two and a desperate battle began.*

Down to the Plains

After the battle in the gorge, the mountain peoples left Hannibal's army alone to struggle wearily on. Each pass they trudged painfully across led to another mountain valley. The path seemed to be always uphill. Many soldiers who fell sick or had been wounded in the battles collapsed and died. At last Hannibal's scouts came back with better news. At the top of the next pass there were no more mountains to climb and the path led downward. A cheer of relief sounded from the cracked throats of the exhausted soldiers.

On the second day of the descent they reached a wide plateau. There they waited for the wounded and the sick to catch up. From the edge of the plateau there was a view across the plains of northern Italy.

Hannibal gathered his weary soldiers together and spoke to them. He praised them for coming through all the dangers they had faced and told them that their reward lay in front of them. In a few days the army would be on those plains. The Gauls of northern Italy would join them, and together they would march south to capture Rome. They would be rich, Italy would be free from Roman rule, and the power of Carthage would rise again.

That night the first snow of winter fell. The next day there was a blizzard. When Hannibal and his army began to move, the path was hidden beneath a thick layer of snow. On the steep and slippery slopes men and animals found it hard to keep their balance. If they fell, they often slid off the path and over the cliffs. Frostbite damaged the feet and fingers of many soldiers. Only the elephants rarely slipped and seemed not to feel the cold.

The march became a grim struggle. Each morning the soldiers had to leave behind the frozen bodies of their friends who had died during the bitter cold of the night. At one place an avalanche had destroyed the path and it took three days to build a ramp to cross the gap. Farther down, a rockfall blocked the way. Huge boulders and tons of rocks rose in a tumbled heap. By heating the rocks with fire and pouring ice-cold water on them, Hannibal's soldiers split them into pieces small enough to move.

When at last they reached the plains, Hannibal's soldiers could do no more. It was lucky that the Romans were not waiting there, ready for battle. The exhausted men needed time to rest and grow strong again before they could face the Roman army.

Toward Rome

Hannibal's brave crossing of the Alps had caught the Romans by surprise. Many of the Gauls in northern Italy rushed to become Hannibal's allies. By the time the Roman legions marched north, Hannibal's soldiers were fit once more, and they moved south to meet the Romans.

The Romans were waiting for Hannibal at the Trebia River. As he had realized when crossing the Rhone River, Hannibal could not move his soldiers over the river safely while enemy troops were on the far bank. This time he hid 2,000 of his soldiers in a hollow by the river bank. Then, as the sun rose, he sent his Numidian cavalry to attack the Roman camp. Although caught by surprise, the Romans quickly fought the Numidians off. As they rode away, the Romans chased them. The Roman leaders thought this was their chance to defeat Hannibal and moved all their legions across the river. In fact this was all part of Hannibal's plan. When the Romans had passed the soldiers' hiding place, Hannibal's army came down to face the legions. At the same moment Hannibal's hidden soldiers attacked the Romans from behind. The legions were surrounded and destroyed.

After his victory Hannibal continued to march south. More legions blocked the way on each coast of Italy. Hannibal decided

Above *The Gauls, who were fearsome enemies camped near the site of Hannibal's river crossing.*

to move between them across the Apennine mountains. Once over the Apennines, Hannibal and his men found themselves struggling through the marshes of the Arno River. For three days the soldiers waded through water that was often waist-deep. Mosquitoes were everywhere, spreading malaria and fever through the army. Sleep was impossible, because the only places to lie down were small tussocks of grass rising out of the swamp. When any of the baggage animals died of exhaustion, the tired soldiers rested on the dead animals' bodies. Hannibal suffered an eye infection and became blind in one eye.

Although the struggle through the marshes had left his soldiers ill and exhausted, Hannibal took the Romans by surprise once more. When the Roman Consul, Flaminius, heard that Hannibal had crossed the marshes he rushed to block the route to Rome with his legions. Hannibal was waiting for Flaminius at Lake Trasimene. As always, Hannibal had planned his battle carefully and the Romans fell into his trap. Caught between Hannibal's soldiers and the waters of the lake, two entire legions were destroyed and Flaminius was killed. Nothing could stop Hannibal from reaching the gates of Rome.

Below *Although it was usual for the victors to strip their dead enemies of armor, weapons and jewelry, Hannibal insisted that the fallen leaders of defeated Roman armies be buried with honor.*

From Victory to Defeat

Triumphantly, Hannibal marched south. He expected the Romans to surrender and ask for peace. Instead they strengthened their city walls and prepared for a siege. Hannibal knew he could not capture Rome; his army was too small to surround the city and he had none of the special weapons needed to break down the walls and gates. He decided that he must persuade Rome's allies in Italy to join him and together they would be able to force Rome to surrender.

As Hannibal marched to the south of Italy, the Romans sent the Consul, Fabius, to follow him with an army of four legions. Fabius decided not to risk a battle but to watch Hannibal until he made a mistake.

Few of Rome's allies joined Hannibal that year. The cities of Italy remembered that Rome had brought peace to a country that had suffered centuries of wars. Hannibal had little to offer except freedom from Rome, and the people of Italy did not really want that freedom.

The next year, 216 BC, the Romans sent out eight legions, twice as many soldiers as Hannibal had. The two armies met at Cannae, and once more, Hannibal destroyed the Roman legions. This time he left the center of his army weaker than usual, and gave his soldiers orders to retreat slowly in front of the mass of Romans.

As the Romans charged forward they found themselves in Hannibal's latest trap. From each side Hannibal's African soldiers attacked the Romans. This time only two of the eight legions escaped, and over 60,000 Roman soldiers were killed.

Above *The site of the Battle of Cannae as it is today.*

Even his crushing victory at Cannae did not bring Hannibal new allies. For another thirteen years Hannibal traveled through Italy with his army. He captured the port of Tarentum and defeated the Romans in many more battles, but it was clear that Rome would not give in. During these years Hannibal and his soldiers lived in the wild mountain forests of Bruttium, in the south of Italy.

Elsewhere, Rome was winning the war with Carthage. In 208 BC Hannibal's brother Hasdrubal was defeated in Spain. The Carthaginians' new empire was conquered by the Roman Consul, Scipio. Hasdrubal then marched over the Alps into Italy, as Hannibal had done ten years earlier. Before he could reach Hannibal, Hasdrubal's army was destroyed by the Roman legions. When Hannibal's youngest brother Mago landed in Italy in 205 BC his army, too, was destroyed by the Romans before he could join Hannibal in Bruttium. In 204 BC the Roman Consul, Scipio, invaded Africa. Hannibal was called back to Carthage to help defend it from Scipio's legions. As he set sail Hannibal knew his dream of defeating Rome was broken.

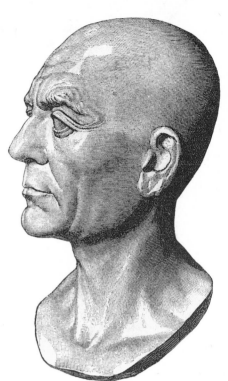

Above *The great Roman leader Scipio Africanus was a young soldier on the losing side at Cannae. He later became one of the few generals ever to gain victory over Hannibal.*

Left *Cannae was the worst defeat ever suffered by the Romans. Despite their heavy losses, the people of Rome refused to surrender to Hannibal. Unable to capture Rome, Hannibal finally had to return to Carthage without achieving his main aim.*

Carthage and Exile

By the time Hannibal reached Africa, Scipio's legions had beaten the Carthaginians in two battles. During the winter of 203 BC there were fierce arguments among the people of Carthage. One group called for an end to the war with Rome. The other, led by Hannibal, said that Carthage's only hope was to fight on. Eventually the people of Carthage took Hannibal's side, and he started training a new army. At the Battle of Zama in 202 BC, Hannibal's new army was defeated. In return for peace the Carthaginians agreed to destroy their warships. They promised never to make war on Rome again, and paid a large sum of money to the Romans.

The war had not prevented Carthaginian merchants from trading, and Carthage was able to pay off its debt to the Romans sooner than expected. As Hannibal grew powerful again the Romans became worried. They were afraid he might want to lead a new battle against Rome. Within Carthage the other ruling families had

Below *At the Battle of Zama, Scipio Africanus finally defeated Hannibal, and Carthage asked for peace. Despite all Hannibal's efforts he had been unable to restore Carthage to its earlier power.*

always been jealous of Hannibal. Now these enemies began to complain to the Romans about Hannibal's power within the city.

One day in 195 BC, Roman envoys arrived at Carthage demanding that Hannibal be sent to Rome to stand trial. Hannibal knew his rivals in Carthage would take this opportunity to betray him. That night he rode to his villa on the coast. A galley was waiting, loaded with members of his family and with money. Hannibal was gone before anyone could stop him, but he was not out of danger yet. The next day his ship stopped at an island to load more food and water. To Hannibal's horror other Carthaginian ships were there. If they knew his plans they might attempt to capture him. He invited all the captains to a feast, suggesting they bring their sails ashore to provide

shade from the sun. Hannibal drank little and the others were soon drunk. While they slept, Hannibal sailed away.

Hannibal spent the rest of his life in exile. At first he lived in Syria at the court of Antiochus the Great. When the Romans defeated Antiochus' army, Hannibal fled to Crete. After some years the Romans conquered Crete, but Hannibal escaped again. The Romans were determined to find Hannibal, and, as their empire grew over the whole Mediterranean, Hannibal was forced farther east. At last, in 183 BC, Hannibal grew tired of running away. He was sixty-four years old and living in Bithynia on the shores of the Black Sea. One night Roman soldiers surrounded his house. Hannibal ended their chase by drinking poison, and when the Romans broke in at dawn he was already dead.

Above *This 19th-century engraving shows Hannibal, exhausted by the Roman pursuit, about to commit suicide by swallowing poison.*

Glossary

Allies Countries, people or organizations that have agreed to work together and help each other.

Avalanche A large mass of snow or rocks that becomes dislodged from a mountain and slides down the slopes.

Bog Soft, muddy ground.

Delta The area of land where a large river meets the sea. It is usually very fertile land.

Dugouts Boats made by hollowing out large tree trunks.

Envoys Official messengers who carry information from one ruler to another.

Foothills The first low hills at the bottom of a range of mountains.

Gauls In the days of Hannibal, Gaul included modern-day France, Belgium, the southern Netherlands and Northern Italy. The people of Gaul were called Gauls. They also lived in northern Spain and Italy.

Mutiny Refusal to obey, as when soldiers refuse to obey their leaders.

Pass A high mountain valley. This valley can be used to cross to the other side of the mountains.

Plateau A broad area of high, level land.

Sacrifice An offering to a god of an animal or human life.

Books to Read

Ancient Rome by Charles Alexander Robinson, Jr. (Franklin Watts, 1984)

Imperial Rome by Jill Hughes (Gloucester, 1985)

Julius Ceasar and the Romans by Robin May (Bookwright, 1985)

Science in Ancient Rome by Jacqueline L. Harris (Franklin Watts, 1988)

See Inside a Roman Town by Jonathan Rutland (Warwick, 1986)

Picture Acknowledgments

Th publishers would like to thank the following for their illustrations: Aldus Archive 5 (top), 20 (bottom); Bridgeman Art Library 8; The Mansell Collection *frontispiece*, 8, 13 (top) 17; Mary Evans 24, 25, 27 (bottom), 28, 29; Peter Newark's Western Americana 6 (right), 27 (top); Ronald Sheridan's Ancient Art and Architecture Collection 5 (bottom), 6 (left), 26; Tony Stone Picture Library 10, 13 (bottom), 20 (top). All maps by Peter Bull.

Finding out More

The Roman Empire eventually covered all of western Europe, including Britain. It also ran along the North African coast and around the shores of the Mediterranean, including much of the Middle East. If you live in, or visit, any of these countries you will probably be able to see sites of Roman buildings and towns. Local museums often stage exhibitions about life in Roman times, but sad to say, little is left of Carthage.

Index